MINING TOWN MEMORIES

Story in Poem

BILLY RAY BIBB

authorHOUSE®

AuthorHouse™
1663 Liberty Drive
Bloomington, IN 47403
www.authorhouse.com
Phone: 1 (800) 839-8640

Published by AuthorHouse 01/18/2019

ISBN: 978-1-5462-7704-0 (sc)
ISBN: 978-1-5462-7702-6 (hc)
ISBN: 978-1-5462-7703-3 (e)

Library of Congress Control Number: 2019900765

MINING TOWN

Memories (Minden, West Virginia)

MINING TOWN Memories

Billy Ray Bibb

A Story in Poem

INTRODUCTION

My mom and dad were married in 1935. Their first home was a wash house attached to a friend's house in the coal-mining town of Minden, West Virginia. My dad worked in the Minden mine for twenty-five years before it closed in the fifties.

I dedicate this book to all
the miners and their families who spent
their lives in the New River Pocahontas
coal-mining town of Minden, West Virginia.

OUR LITTLE TOWN, MINDEN

Have you ever been in our darling little town of
Minden,
where many coal miners and families lived and
died in?

Our company home was good enough to live in,
although the cracks in the walls would let the
wind,
rain, and snow in.

A $2 script book on the half weekend equaled two
bags of groceries
to carry its worth in.

A bathtub hardly big enough to get your feet in
is where we bathed on the weekend.

1

Even though we always had enough food to eat,
there was not always our favorite meat.

Our hillside garden supplied its fair share;
all the aches and pains we would all come to bear.

About all of this we really didn't care;
it was all the love we found in folks who lived
there.

God blessed our darling little town of Minden,
where many miners and families lived and died in,
and He does today as He did then.

God bless our little town of Minden!

08-02-2013

A MINER'S PRAYER

Be with me as I enter Mother Earth today.
Hold her steady as I mine coal, I pray.
Keep me in your tender loving care.
Protect me as I travel to my work down there.
Keep my thoughts on you as we leave fresh air,
As daylight turns to dust and darkness down there.
Every shift requires on-the-job and faithful concentration,
Being very aware of any movement and sensation.
Keeping my mind aware of any change there
Helps me feel what I need to do to prepare.
A constant prayer on my lips each hour of the day
Assures me of the safe return to my family, I pray.

08-03-2015

CHILDREN OF THE MINE

Taken from the rooms of primary school
To the rolling belt of coal to set upon a stool,
Sorting slate from the lumps of black gold,
Enduring the dark, dank days down there so cold.
Children started a life there in the mine
That shaped their mining careers in kind.
This work is done by machine today;
Now the children can learn, run, and play.

03-2015

THE YOUNG MINER

It wasn't easy for a new couple
To start a life without any trouble.
Getting a paying job in the mine
Took a great deal of patience and time.
Once this could support a married man.
There arose many obstacles before the plan.
Not only the expense of the two,
A matter of housing was one of the few
To consider in a bustling coal-mining town.
Your job status played a role, but do not frown.
There were other possibilities in the town,
Such as renting or using someone's wash
House, not very accommodating or posh.
It may be a parents' home attached.
But otherwise, you would need to put up cash.

I recall one couple cleaned out a chicken barn.
An unlikely place to live, you might say, but darn,
It's a start in a bustling coal-mining town
When there was no place to go but down.
Some mining towns had lodging in boarding homes.
You could rent a room or two if you could
Afford the cost; your company pay would make it good.
Payday came and went, didn't mean you got a cent.
The coal company got its due before you had a clue.
What do you use for food and pay other things due?
The company was always there for you!
We will put it on your company store bill to see you through!
"St. Peter, don't call me 'cause I can't go,
I owe my soul to the company store."

02-16-2016

A TRIBUTE TO THE MINER

Put yourself in the place of a miner
Who left his wife and children today
To work way down the mine for little pay.
The dank, dark, wet air way down there
Makes a man wonder why he wants to be here.
What would send a man to risk his life there,
Rattling timbers, black coal dust in the air?
Shifting, rumbling of the rooftop up there
Sends shivers up your spine, which we all share.
Our very existence relies on our work there—
The food we eat, the roofs over our heads,
A place for our wives and children to make their
beds.
I can't imagine a life in the mine so despair
Could bring any happiness for families to share.

Could you put yourself in this mind-set?

Even though so comfortable, so peaceful we get,

Coal miners suffered so much for our progress.

Let's remember and revere their lives for our success.

God bless the miner—grandfathers, fathers, and sons.

08-17-2014

Spirit of the Miner

Their lives were lost in a place so low
We wonder what must become of their souls.
When tragedy comes and loved ones go,
We grieve many years, wanting to know.
The day when a blast occurs there,
Or the top cracks and caves in where
The miner is working, so dark and dank,
Makes us wonder what they felt, would think.
My life may be at hand this day.
What will my wife, children, and family say
To my leaving them when I came to work today
To earn a living for food and a place for them to
stay?
So for the lost miner, let's continue to pray.

03-2015

11

A MINER GOES TO HEAVEN

A miner thought he died and went to heaven,
Meeting head on with St. Peter, who asked, "No reservation?"
The miner said, "Well, it was a spur of the moment thing.
It was a usual day in the mine; my head began to ring.
I went into the mine in the light of day,
Finding the workplace, I took a turn and lost my way.
I came upon a crowd of what looked like heavenly host.
They were weeping and moaning over what looked like a ghost.

A tune, something like, 'Sixteen tons, and what do you get,'
Came from the crowd of floating beings, and yet,
As I came nearer, I began to fret.
The ghost looked a lot like someone I had met.
The closer I got, the clearer I could see.
You know, that miner looked a lot like me.
I told St. Peter I wasn't ready quite yet.
He said, 'You created this mess; it's what you get.
Instead of the rumbling and cracking of the mine,
It was the stress of life and cracking of your mind.
No need to stay here,' he said, 'Now get.
Your reservation has not been confirmed as of yet.
I think the wife will be waiting at home, I expect,
To see how much coal you mined today
And how much script for food you have in pay.
I know the work of a miner is rough to make each day,
But if you must die, you will know there is a better way.
Oh, and one thing more, and it's for sure,
You still owe your soul to the company store!'"

03-15-2015

THE MINER AND BLACK LUNG

The young miner works every day, you see,
planning his life and providing for his family,
each day working in the heavy black air
to mine coal car by car to total up his share.
Conditions beneath the dark dank ground down
there
don't provide a healthy source of proper air.
The atmosphere down there contains impurities
that stay in a man's lungs. you see.
Day in, day out, breathing this mixed-up air
must certainly bring a man's health some despair.
As days, weeks, months, and years go by,
a man's body will be deprived of oxygen to live by;
his lungs lose capacity to breathe, deprived
of this necessary function, to survive.

This means of making a living is a real distress
compared to what it means to live in happiness.
So the life and health of the miner, you see,
is not the kind of life we should want it to be.
A means of providing for himself and family
is the goal of a coal miner, you see!

Black lung and silicosis kill many West Virginia
coal miners as do many unsafe working conditions.
Let's remember all these brave men who provided
a means to fire plants and provide many products
and resources throughout the industrialized world.

Thank the miner for bringing a greater light to the
world from such a damp, dank, dark place. Thank
you. May God bless you.

WHEN THE WHISTLE BLOWS

When the whistle at the mine blows
And blows and blows until everyone knows
There has been an incident at the mine.
Everyone runs to the mine, asking, "Was it mine,
Was it my husband involved in the cave-in?"
"Was it my husband?" another wife would whine.
Everyone very excited and scared for lives.
All the families in the coal camp and wives
Gather at the mine, which may last one day,
maybe one night, maybe several days, they say.
"Was it an explosion?" one may ask another,
"Or did the roof cave in on my brother?"
The time is long and restless as time goes on
through the day and through the night to the
rising sun.

Little or no word has come to those who wait.

Minds run amok; prayers go up at such a gait.

Then finally, the word comes from the section boss.

Some men are hurt, but thank God none were lost.

Many a miner was lost in just this way,

so to the many, let us continue to pray, no loss today.

May God bless the miners and families who experienced a scene such as this.

I dedicate this poem to our lost Minden miners.
07-20-2015

THE MINE IS GONE

I'm sure by now you all know
The mine is gone forever, and so
What's left to feed our memories?
Well, there's the memory of the mine, and let's see.

The miners lost are always in our memories.
The families left behind deserve our respect.
Of course, many are getting older I expect,
And their children are not far behind.
We need to keep their children in mind.
Of course, you might expect by now
Their knowledge of all this is a little, "Like wow!"
Ask yourself, "Would they know what a mine is?"
"What did it do? Why should I remember?" they
whine.

Is it really my place to continue to do this?

Well, I guess it could be amiss,

An opportunity to carry on the past,

Just like all other events in our history.

"To keep it alive?" you ask.

Yes, and for as long as we have memory.

By the way, what is "coal"?

What does it look like? Do you remember?

When was the last time you saw a lump of coal?

08-29-2015

Jesse James, the Motor Running Man

The motor was to become part of him was his
plan.
He would run his motor car as fast as he can,
No more in the mine, with no cars on the track,
In a flash here he came, pulling many cars back.
This was his goal for the entire shift,
As quick as a flash to be very thrift.
His coworkers said they never saw anyone so fast.
He relied on them to make this routine last.
Without this cooperation of the crew team,
Production at this rate would run out of steam.
Coal mining took many forms over the years,
From donkeys and ponies to pull cars with the
load

To heavy, iron, electric motors of the towing mode.
The first coal cars were pushed by the miner,
And to make a better pay, the family would enter
The mine, a desolate, dark, dank place to render
Endless shifts to make a living of the lowest form.
This life, such as it was, became the norm.
Jesse James, the motor running man, was bad.
I don't say this just because he was my dad.
I believe his real goal was to spend more time outside
Rather than inside the mine
And as little as possible inside in kind.
I guess this would provide some blessed peace,
Possibly avoiding some danger at least.

11-07-2015

THE MINER'S FAMILY

We had a pretty big family, you see.
There were Mom, Dad, five sisters,
two brothers, and me.
Life must have been pretty sweet back then,
When only one or two children were in the den.
As each year went by, an addition to the crew,
Added at least one, almost one time nearly two.
Dad working the night shift in the mine,
Mom working three shifts actually full time,
Life became more tense, and
tempers would flare.
It seemed like control in the
household took shares.
Mom said, "I will manage the girls, you see."
Dad said, "I will manage the boys. Hee!"

This was a very sad time in the boys' life.
Dad's frustration with our
behavior became strife.
Next thing we knew, talk no longer exists.
I felt at times it would become fists to fists.
But no, the miners bank belt would rule.
If chores were not done, it was use the tool.
After many lashes you would know
Which side you were on, or where
the strips would show.
Once while Dad was sleeping, a
scary movie we had watched,
Caused a commotion when I spooked
my sisters and got caught.
That caused me to get it so bad I don't remember
Breathing again for what seemed
like November or December.
The miner's whole family shared
this life, as you can see.
Lord, if you hadn't blessed this
family, where would we be?

05-27-2015

Our Big Lump of Coal

We lived in many company
houses in Minden Town.
Although many have burned or
have been torn down,
I counted seven at one time or another you see.
This one we lived in made us a coal company.
It was at the end of a row of company houses,
On one of those company numbered hills,
Where one day a big sinkhole brought on chills.
It was at the end of the road at the turnaround,
Not too far from where a big lump
of coal would be found.

Since Dad was buying the land
where a large hole abound,
The reality company said, "We
are willing to compensate
By giving you something to put food
on the family dinnerplate.
There is a large lump of coal
you can have, you see,
To compensate for the loss of land
created by the coal company."
Don't you know, we just
became a coal company.
The old Dodge truck hauled many tons of coal,
Sold throughout Minden Town
to nearly every soul.
We boys would load the wheelbarrow,
and to the truck we would go.
It took thirteen loads to make a ton and so,
Until our mine would become so
dangerous from the top, you know.
There were many tons of yellow
dirt above our heads.

Mom became very worried and said
Our mine was going to be shut down,
Just like the big mine in Minden Town.

05-27-2015

Union Hall Memories

From miners to soldiers, many
from Minden back then
Went to war in World War II and
served their countrymen.
While growing up, trips to the
Minden Union Hall
Would prove to quite an experience, I recall.
I remember seeing a tattered, old
US flag high upon the wall.
As the story goes, I was told it was brought back
To our coal-mining town to serve
as a reminder of the attack.
It flew at the liberation by our soldiers
In the town of Minden, Germany,
put upon their shoulders.

Many times the union would give Christmas
Treats to the miners' children
at Christmastime for us.
It was usually a brown paper
bag with some treats,
Like candy, fruits, and nuts; we
didn't often get sweets.
The Miners Union would provide
food supplements when
The miners would strike for higher wages
or when there was no work back then.
There could be long times; they
couldn't work, you see,
So many had to find some means
to feed their family,
Many times as children we were
sent to the union hall
To carry food home on a wagon or sled; we all
Got together, very excited to
accomplish the haul.
Several of us kids would do this together.
It didn't matter what the weather,

We all loved to ride the sled
anyway when snow came.
It always brings back fond
memories just the same.

06-04-2015

Berry-Picking Time

In the summertime, around July,
Picking blackberries always caught our eye.
All of us kids of any useful size
Would climb up the hills toward
the Pea Ridge side,
Where most likely all the best
bushes would hide.
From our home on our coal company hill
Toward Captain Thurmond's
Cemetery was our will.
Mom canned fruit and berries;
many jars we did fill.
She said, "These will make many
warm treats to beat the

chill."
When winter came, these
summer chores provided a
tasty thrill.
Mom was soon happy with all she could can.
So then it was the kids' turn to make their plan.
From then on, as long as they lasted you see,
We sold blackberries to the coal
camp and company.
As other wild fruit trees in the
woods would bear,
We gathered as much as we
could to get our share.
Apples, peaches we did find.
Not all were the suitable canning kind,
So Mom said, "We'll just make
jam and jelly, you see.
These things were provided, you
know, just not perfectly."
This was a regular event for us
kids after school was out.

We could do this and have plenty
of fun rousting about.
When chores were done, it
was down to the creek.
The water was so cold it made us shriek.

06-04-2015

CHRISTMAS IN MINDEN TOWN

Christmastime in Minden Town
didn't mean a lot of tinsel and glitter around.
A few clear window candles could be seen.
We didn't experience the modern Christmas scene.
Roaming the ravines between Minden and
Thurmond hills,
we usually brought home a three sided-piney thrill.
One side or two would always be hidden by the
corner wall,
but it seemed to bring out the holiday thrill in all.
I remember making a Christmas scene display,
A white house and church with lights inside
to light the windows and doors to our delight.
Set on white cotton to resemble some snow,
covered with glitter to reflect the light, you know.

Those old orange crates from the company store
made these things possible for sure.
Regifting wasn't anything new back then.
Something old may be wrapped up within
some Christmas paper from a year ago.
Still a gift for everyone, so, "Ho! Ho! Ho!"
Mom always baked a lot for this time of year.
Fruitcake, cookies, fudge, and cinnamon buns were some
of the festive foods we managed to have at home.
The central place of most Christmas cheer
was in the company store this time of year.
The second story area was Toyland; what a delight
to see all the wonderful toys and bright lights.
It was great to visit there, you see.
But it didn't mean we would get anything from there under our tree.
Maybe one gift or so, and maybe nuts and candy.
So we were blessed to have our family.

Merry Christmas.

07-21-2015

MOMA, BACK IN THE DAY

Moma stayed at home all the day,

making biscuits for us in the morning and pray,

washing clothes and hanging them on the line,

working between two crosses all the time.

Songs she would sing all the day;

you know, the Lord heard her pray.

Swinging her babies on the porch swing,

you could always hear her sing

"In the Sweet By and By"

until they would no longer cry.

Uniform of the day was the apron she wore,

and to raise a blessed family was her chore.

She would be blessed forever more

as this was a family she would adore.

There was nothing in this world she would want more.

11-06-2014

Mother's Old Porcelain Coffeepot

There's not much left to treasure from our meager
home.
Most things we may have been cherished are now
gone.
Not many things of value resided in our family
home.
Only one thing remains today we can reflect upon.
I remember it sitting in the old china closet where
Mother
kept it there,
where it stayed most of our childhood, handled
with the
best of care.
A gift to Mother from Dad, you see,

upon the birth of their third daughter to be.
It was given to her before Mother passed away;
It sets in her home now, where it will stay.
Seventy years ago, a part of our home it would play.
A single family heirloom is still here today.

Falling from Grace

"The Look"

Through life we had nothing to fear,
but should you fall from grace,
it would appear ...
The Look!

We were not physically punished, you might say,
but still we didn't get away without ...
The Look!

It sent us to our retreat—a room, a corner,
or even our little chair—brought on by ...
The Look!

It was ours throughout life to bear, our

punishment would scare us to repentance.

There were no words, no argument to repair,
only "The Look" that would scare.

2010

THE CHOIR CLOUD

Sitting on the porch of my West Virginia home,
Some amazing clouds in the
sky came floating by.
A number of what looked like angels shone.
Big wings and long, flowing
gowns caught my eye.
They were perfectly aligned as they could be,
As if they might be ready to sing to me.
The wind pushed them in perfect array.
I thought they were there, some time to stay.
So content, I watched them gradually go away,
Wishing that much longer they could stay.
It was a beautiful blue sky that day.

White wind–swept clouds in
such a beautiful way.
We get a view of what heaven may display,
How beautiful things we may see there one day.

05-27-2015

FRUIT OF THE VINE

Heavenly Father, you are the vine of the of the
fruit we know.
From the branch of the vine we all grow.
From the wine of the fruit its juice will flow
With the joy of the presence of its sweet glow.
Lives are sustained by its presence here below,
Not to be abused by its spirits we know.
Your example of this we hope to show.
Each time it represents the blood of your Son,
Who gave his life for our sins we know.
Thank you, God, that you love us so
To give your Son to death on the cross so low.

05-20-2015

THE BERRY AND THE HOLLY TREE

Glory be, you know God created this holly tree.

He created a redbird to be here with me.

Its song sounds so very pretty.

I wish I could be a big holly tree.

And just then, that redbird took a bite and swallowed me.

I guess this will be the end of me

And my wish to be a big holly tree.

Then all of a sudden, I felt free.

Out of that bird I came, and I could see.

I hit the ground, and glory be,

The dirt covered over the top of me.

There I was, buried deep.

I felt so bad, I began to weep.

And then I felt roots growing out of me.

A big green spear shot up out of me.

Up and up it grew, so big and free,

I knew then I was going to be a great big holly tree.

A redbird came to sit and began to sing to me.

Its song sounded so very pretty.

For now you see, God made me what I wished I could be,

A great big holly tree.

11-06-2014

SCRAPPERS' CORNER

Can't you just imagine what went on
When someone said to another, "Let's get it on!"
A dispute of one kind or another;
It may have been with one's brother,
It could have started and boiled over
To the old center of all disputes, Scrappers' Corner.
Could it have started at the local pub,
Spilling over all the way down Minden Hill
To the center of dispute, where it was their will,
To settle their differences and still,
It could have started on Old Minden Road,
And reservations were made to settle
A little ways down the road right in the middle?
I'm sure some disgruntled miners found

Reason to grumble over dissatisfied conditions underground.

A lady could be the center of anyone's location,

Folks from Concho or Rocklick on occasion.

Maybe Daisy Hill or Dog Hollow disputes in that day

May have boiled over, could wind up that way.

Up to old Scrappers' Corner was the order of the day,

To put this old, nagging dispute at bay.

08-29-2015

THE SPIRIT OF WEST VIRGINIA

The spirit of West Virginia lies deep beneath the hills.

Many have come to work here to fill its tills.

They came here from many lands to work here below

To seek their fortune and make it here, you know.

Many countries worldwide gave up their able men,

Who traveled far and wide to work here within.

A meager life they found to accommodate them.

Many gave their lives and remain in the hills within

Whom creates the spirit of West Virginia mining men.

03-2015

It's Old, but It's New

The oldest river in the Western
Hemisphere is called The New.
There are not many like it, only a few.
It winds through the mountains
of WV and out to the shore,
Rolling through green valleys with
white water rapids that roar.
It travels along many mining
camps; it's a sight to see,
Bringing boating, white-water rafting,
and flooding occasionally.
It's said by many it has a
shifting bottom, you see,
With big, dark, deep holes
there are thought to be.

Legend has it a long coal train
one day met its destiny,
Running off the rails, plunging
in the water, you see,
To the shifting bottom, wherever that may be.
To this day, no one knows when
or if we may ever see
The legendary coal train that met its destiny.

05-27-2015

DADDY'S GRACE

Bless this food,
its tender goodness,
and our lives to thy service.
Feed us on the bread of life,
and save us for Christ's sake.

Amen.

2008

West Virginia Gals

West Virginia gals are mighty fine.
They are the best of the marrying kind.
Their long, flowing auburn hair
frames a gal that is mighty fair;
makeup and eye shadow come natural out there.
One shift in the mine will meet that bill of fare.
West Virginia gals don't leave home to get a beau;
trapped in the mine, there's no place to go.
Mountain cookin' from a gal so good lookin'
provides a life not forsookin'.

THE LEAF AND ME, I

One day, the weather turned cold,

And the sap went down.

All of a sudden, my leaf turned brown.

From the top of the tree, I came falling down,

Whirling and tumbling to the ground.

What will become of me from now on?

I lay among many others like me,

All in a heap to meet my destiny.

I'll crumble and disintegrate

If the air stays dry; but if it's wet,

I'll turn to brown mulch and wait

To be sucked up by the vacuum

Monster that will come along,

Only to spit and blow me around
To a garden in the spring,
Bringing forth many new renderings.

03-03-15

THE LEAF AND ME, II

I was a thriving leaf in the top of my tree.
I was green and alive as life could be.
Then all at once, life seemed to flee.
My tree turned off life on me.
I guess this is called life's season change,
But when this happened, my life was rearranged.
It was a beautiful fall day when the wind swept
me away,
Hurling and twirling, this and that way.
I now lie flat and all brown,
Wet and decaying upon the ground.
That tree sure has let me down.
I guess in life what goes up must come down.

03-03-2015

MOUNTAIN AIR

There's something to be said about mountain air.
You can't find it just anywhere.
It's up there for all to share.
It's in the trees of green,
As green as you've ever seen.
Between the ridges and the grass so green,
The mountain air is so clean.

11-06-2014

MY HOBBY

As a young boy, I liked to work with wood.

So off to the company store I went as often as I
could

To get many wooden orange crates for wood.

I would very carefully take them apart, you see,

To salvage all the nice pieces of wood for me

To make a lot of model wooden wagons, my hobby.

They ranged from covered wagons, stagecoaches,

Buggies, freight wagons, a fire wagon were the
most.

While working at the company store in its last
days,

A friend and I would help Mr. Miller in many
ways.

We would sweep the floor and stock the shelves.

It seemed to us boys we were workingmen.

Upon the shelf something caught my eye just then.

A jigsaw I noticed and said, "I must buy."

Cutting spokes in wheels was hard to do by hand,

But the jigsaw would fit in my plan.

Sawing spokes out in the wheel,

You drill a hole for the jig blade to make them look real.

My hobby kept me busy, you might say.

It brought a sense of joy to many a dreary day.

11-09-2015

MY FIRST BIKE

While walking with my brother from
Mrs. Bates's candy store one day,
An old bike lay over by the railroad
tracks in the tall grass and hay.
I said, "I wonder if that old bike could be mine."
After asking what it cost, it was a matter of time.
It was a pitiful looking bike, you see,
Was all rusted, beat up, and had no tires.
Well, after paying ten dollars for it,
my plans were to ride it at all costs.
Well, that was only a wish, I admit.
My paper route made no cash, only debt.
Selling vegetables was no better bet.
Working Mrs. Moran's garden, same way;
mostly kept me occupied for the day.

While shopping at our local city dump,
I found an interesting item and a tire pump.
A couple of discarded gasoline pump hoses
caught my eye, and I asked, "Do you suppose
they would work on the old bike rims?"
Well, after cutting them, they seemed to fit.
A piece of pipe put them together,
a lot of wire wound around, and that was it.
They made considerable noise, but down the road
it went.
Many miles were put on those tires, you see,
until a good friend gave his old bike to me.

I dedicate this poem to Joel Evans who gave me
a beautiful Roadmaster bike when he gave up
riding. Thanks, Joel.

07-22-2015

Collins High School, Fiftieth Anniversary, 1965

Upon completing the eighth grade at Minden,
About one third of our class began a new life.
Our world was about to change, and so
Everything that our world was not here below.
Good grades were very much what we were used to,
But it became very hard work just to make it we
knew.
After the freshman year was through,
Made it, failing half-semester English, and "Whew."
A change of plans was in order, and soon,
Sophomore year found me on the vocational track.
To shop I would go two thirds of the day; what
the heck,

Many hours of drafting, welding, and machine shop.

I was determined to finish here before I would stop.

English lit. and government would prove the next feat.

But after pacifying Mrs. Bishop with a poem so sweet

To pass one semester and a replica of the Shakespeare's

Theater, I was there to compete.

On to a world I knew nothing about, you see.

Summer of '65 would see me drafted into the army.

Happy fiftieth anniversary, Collins High Class of 1965.

08-31-2015

Our Little Town of Minden Memories

Our little town of Minden, where
Our childhood memories we found there,
I rode my bike from one end
of town to the other,
Sometimes with my friend and
sometimes with my brother.
Our orders were to stay in the yard,
But to obey was very hard.
We were sometimes allowed outside to play
But only for a few hours each day.
Blackberry time we went a pickin',
And if we didn't behave, we got a lickin'.
Seems like our chores were never done,
But we always managed to have some fun.

Our family members numbered ten.
As that was a lot of mouths to feed,
We went to bed hungry often.
The outhouse was way up on the hill.
But as winter came, we got a thrill
As we would sleigh ride very fast down that hill.

07-29-2016

HIS LOVING HANDS

My Father loves me as only He can.

He took time to mold me with His loving hands.

Just imagine God by the creek bed,

On hands and knees, just like He said,

"I made you in My image, you see,

So you might be just like Me.

Shaping every feature there in kind,

That you might serve Me with heart and mind.

This piece of clay molds so easily,

Formed in love and kindness just like me.

I bring forth new life that you may teach

Those who follow my commandments to reach

The divine life to eternity.

Go into the world with love and serenity,
Feel the hands of God upon your face,
Molded in kind to live in this place."

06-19-2016

ODE TO THE OUTHOUSE

Living in a coal company house was not such a thrill.
But one free service that came with it was the
Small white house trimmed in black upon the hill.
This service was provided to each house, you see.
There was no cost; you might say, it was a free utility.
The cold days of winter made it a lonesome trek
To muster up the courage to go sit upon its deck.
The wooden boards that formed the frosty throne
Would make a body tremble and groan.
Thank the Lord for a very small reprieve;
It was the chamber pot, so ill conceived.
This became a deterrent in the warm you see,
To sit upon that marvel in all ecstasy.

Of course, in time this vessel one would have to empty,

So it was someone's job to make the trek

To the little white house trimmed in black, you see.

I dedicate this marvelous writing to my sister Helen, who joked about this experience so joyfully. Many laughs, sis. With all our love.

04-18-2016

To Walk with the Lord

Wonder what it would be like to walk with the
Lord maybe a mile or so, you see.
Would He be taller than me?
Would His gown be glowingly bright?
Could you hear His sandals squeak?
What would it be like?
Could you bear to keep from looking or taking a
peek?
You probably would want to stop and look
In amazement, and let your mind seek
The awesome, radiant feeling of being with Him.
Just the feeling of the radiant love He would
command.
Would His gown leave static sparks on the sand?
The warm feeling and sweet perfume there

Would command sensational love in the air.
How could one man have all this to share?
Could you find all this in your own son?
Wouldn't it be great to possess this love, where
Only God could create this very One
To be all this and allow His life to share
With all who love Him and their every care.

11-06-2016

Hopes and Dreams

A just-enlisted marine lies in his hospital bed after discovering he has a disability and may not be able to complete basic training. He writes this poem of desperation.

The dreams we dream can be fulfilled
If when we dream, we also build.
And we can build the dreams we choose
Depending on the tools we use.
If we would build to greater heights,
We have to raise our hopes and sights.
When hopes and sights are only small,
We can't build lofty, high, and tall.
Thoughts must be big for big success.
Why be content with something less?

Sights must be high if we build high.
But faith has wings,
So why not fly?
To see your hopes and dreams come true,
Think big—think high—
Think good—think new!
The years can see them all fulfilled
By how you think
And how you build.

Christopher Allen Bibb

DOWN AT THE RIVER

You know the river is the lowest

Place here on earth, you see.

Closest to hell here on earth as we can be.

When John baptized Jesus,

He plunged into hell that day,

Coming forth into the light again

In the most wonderful way.

Dying on the cross and to the depths of hell,

Resurrected on the third day, he would live again

to tell.

This is the symbolism of the death

and resurrection our Lord performed

for us to see what a price He paid

for you and me, so forlorn.

The dove descended on Him that day.

This is how God chose to anoint Him this way.

04-21-2017

WAS IT GOD'S PLAN?

God's first son was Adam,
Who also had great effect on the world.
Along with a gal named Eve, his madam,
Who was lost to the devil, you might say,
When he and Eve gave Adam an apple one day.
A wonderful, beautiful world was changed
From this to one with many diverse demands.
Labor would be required to live each day
To provide food and shelter by their hands.
Their eyes were opened to all by Eve's melee,
The day Eve and Satan made this play.
Well, many years passed when upon that day
God sent His second Son to teach His Word
And His love to all here below, you might say.
This Son would be the Savior of the world

To teach the Word of God to all those who may
Believe in Him, love Him, and each day pray
To keep His commandments every day.

04-21-2017

About the Author

Billy Ray, that was the name my Mom chose for me. The doctor said his name on the birth certificate will be William. I'm sure she was dissappointed and had a few choice of words for him at that time ofcourse. I was always called Billy Ray by all the family from that day to this.

As I got older and went out inlo the world, that name would have to go. So when I enlisted into the Navy, I thought Bill may be more approprate. Then I met my wife's family.

I kept Bill as I thought Billy Ray might not be good there either. Although, some of her family had some southerly names with Lee, Ray, Bob And Joe as middle names as well, I felt nearly at home.

I have for sometime had a desire to tell our life's story. It has been eating on me for a number of years now. Finally giving in and wrote these poems from our life's memories.

This became an effort to raise some funds in the beginning for the Minden Communrty Center to preserve some of the town's history. Well, we managed to sell a few same as dollars a few!

Printed in the United States
By Bookmasters